THE HEART

Our Circulatory System

SEYMOUR SIMON

SCHOLASTIC INC.
New York Toronto London Auckland Sydney

Photography Note

Scientists are using fantastic new machines that peer inside the human body to picture the invisible and help doctors save lives. In this book, we see extraordinary views of a beating heart in action, red blood cells pushing through tiny capillaries no bigger than a human hair, and white blood cells surrounding and destroying germs. Many of these images were taken by various kinds of scanners, which change X-ray photos into computer code to make clear, colorful graphics. The computer-enhanced pictures of planets beamed back to Earth from distant space use a similar technique. These new ways of seeing help all of us to understand and appreciate that most wonderful machine: the human body.

To Jeanette Carlson, with heartfelt thanks. The author also thanks Raymond Matta, M.D., for his careful reading of the manuscript of this book and Richard D. Capriotti, M.D., for providing research materials for the artwork.

PHOTO AND ART CREDITS
Permission to use the following photographs is gratefully acknowledged: page 5, Howard Sochurek; page 7, Mehau Kulyk/Science Photo Library; page 10, VU/David M. Phillips; page 13, Professors P. M. Motta and S. Correr/Science Photo Library; pages 14–15, VU/T. Kuwabara and D. Fawcett; pages 16, 32, VU/Fred Hossler; page 21, Science VU/Visuals Unlimited; pages 23, 31, Howard Sochurek/Medical Images; page 25, Don Fawcett and E. Shelton/Science Photo Library; page 27, P. M. Motta/Department of Anatomy, University La Sapienza, Rome/Science Photo Library; page 29, CNRI/Science Photo Library.
Art on pages 9 and 19 by Ann Neumann.

The text type is 18-point Garamond Book.

ISBN 0-590-13091-9

 Published by Scholastic Inc., 555 Broadway, New York, NY 10012, by arrangement with William Morrow & Company, Inc.

12 11 10 9 8 7 6 5 4 3 2 1 7 8 9/9 0 1 2/0

Printed in the U.S.A. 08

First Scholastic printing, September 1997

To Chloe Jacquelyn with love from Grandpa

Make a fist. This is about the size of your heart. Sixty to one hundred times every minute your heart muscles squeeze together and push blood around your body through tubes called blood vessels.

Try squeezing a rubber ball with your hand. Squeeze it hard once a second. Your hand will get tired in a minute or two. Yet your heart beats every second of every day. In one year your heart beats more than thirty million times. In an average lifetime a heart will beat over 2,000,000,000 (two thousand million) times.

The heart works hard when we relax or sleep and even harder when we work or exercise. It never stops for rest or repair. The heart is a most incredible pump.

In this computer-enhanced photograph, the heart is pictured in the center of the chest surrounded by blood vessels in the lungs, neck, and arms.

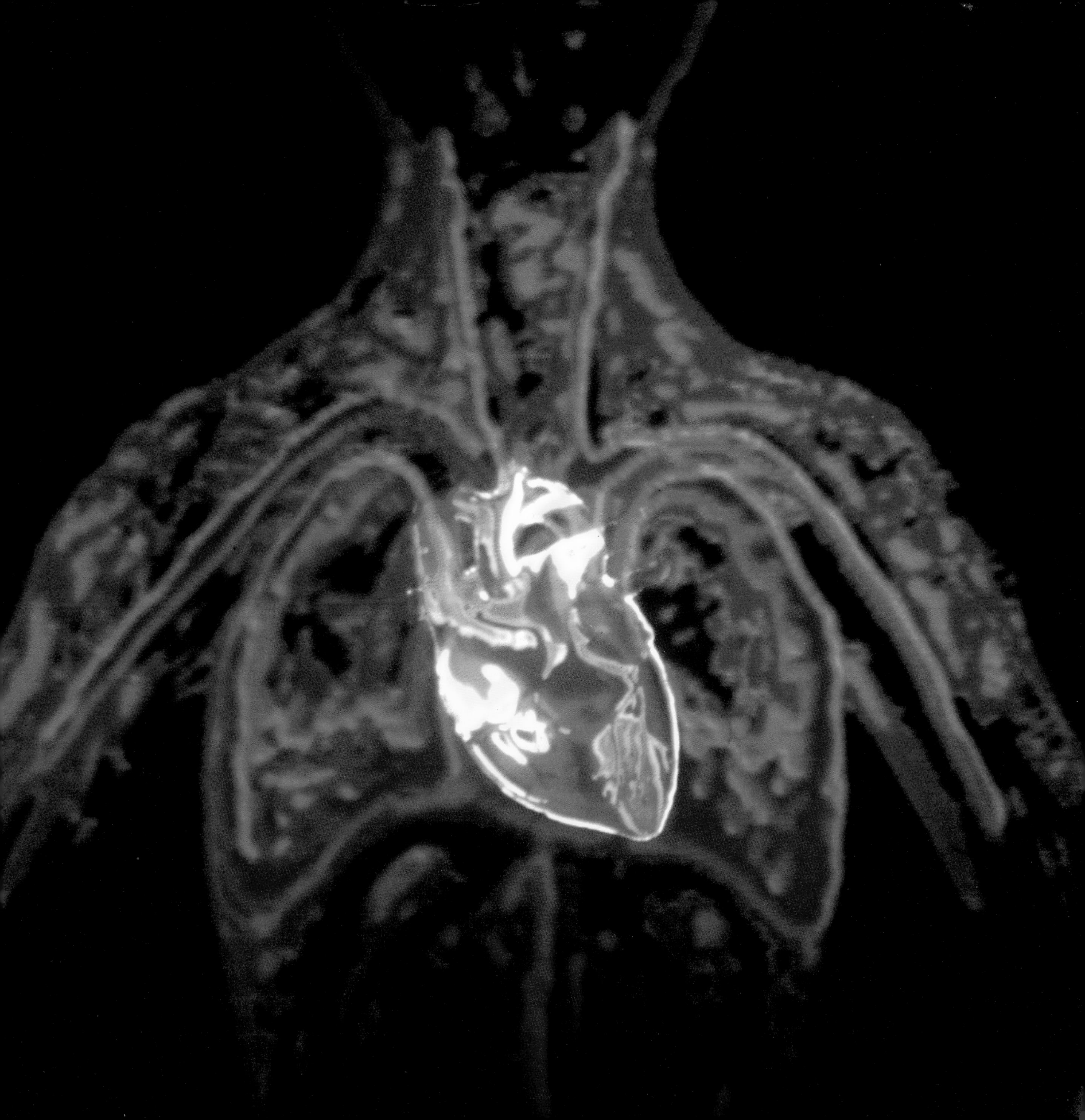

Not all animals have hearts. There are tiny creatures in oceans and ponds that take in food and oxygen from the surrounding waters. But in humans and other mammals, most of the cells lie too deep within the body to get food and oxygen directly from the outside.

The human body is made up of hundreds of billions of microscopic cells. Your muscles, nerves, skin, and bones are all made of different kinds of cells. But every cell in your body needs food and oxygen, and your cells also need to be protected against germs that can cause disease.

Your heart, blood vessels, and blood work together to supply each of your cells with all of its needs. Every minute, the heart pushes a pulsing stream of blood through a network of blood vessels to every cell in your body. The constantly moving blood brings food and oxygen to each cell, carries away such wastes as carbon dioxide, and serves as an important component in the body's immune system. The heart, blood, and web of blood vessels make up your circulatory system.

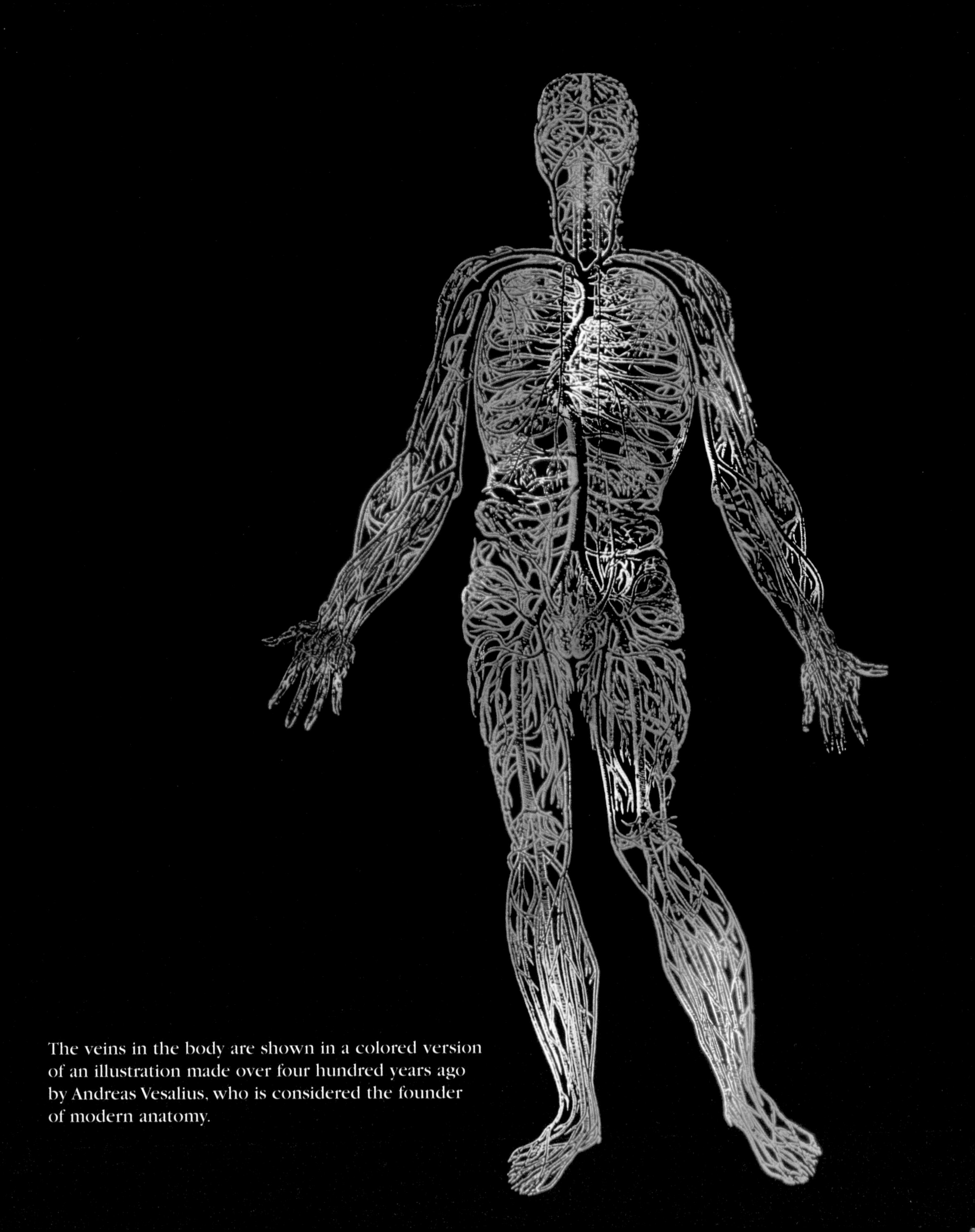

The veins in the body are shown in a colored version of an illustration made over four hundred years ago by Andreas Vesalius, who is considered the founder of modern anatomy.

Your heart is in the middle of your chest, tilted slightly to the left. It weighs only about ten ounces, about as much as one of your sneakers. It is divided into two halves by a thick wall of muscle called the septum, and each side has two hollow chambers, one above the other. Blood enters the heart in the atria, which then pump it down to the lower chambers. Each atrium has a one-way valve that opens when the blood is pushed to the ventricles and then closes so the blood can't flow backward.

The ventricles, the lower chambers of the heart, are heavier and stronger than the atria. The muscular right ventricle pumps blood into the lungs. The even more muscular left ventricle pumps blood to every cell in the body, from the head to the toes. Each ventricle also has a one-way valve to prevent blood from going backward.

Oxygen-poor blood from the body enters and fills the right atrium. At the same time, oxygen-rich blood from the lungs enters and fills the left atrium.

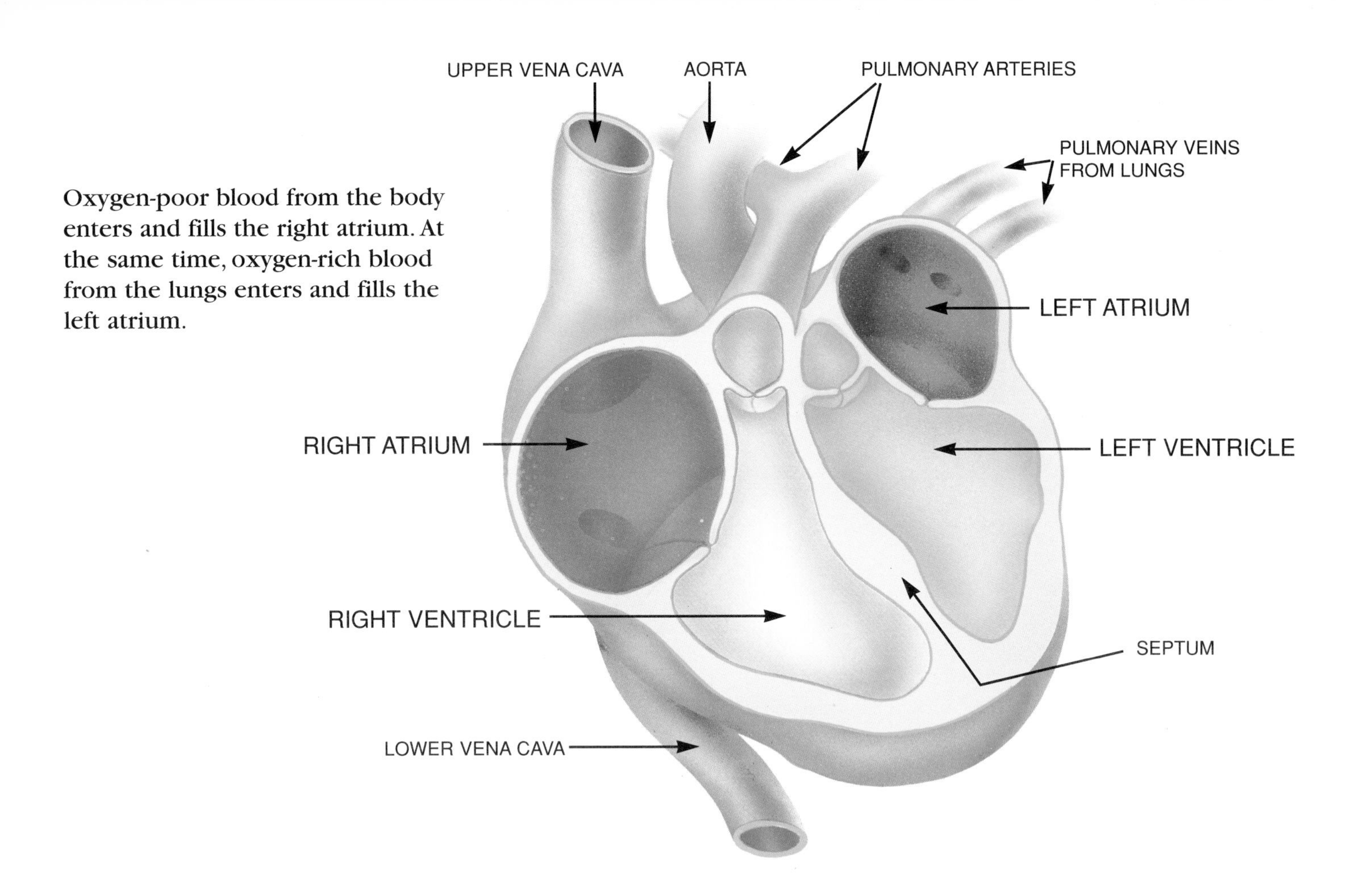

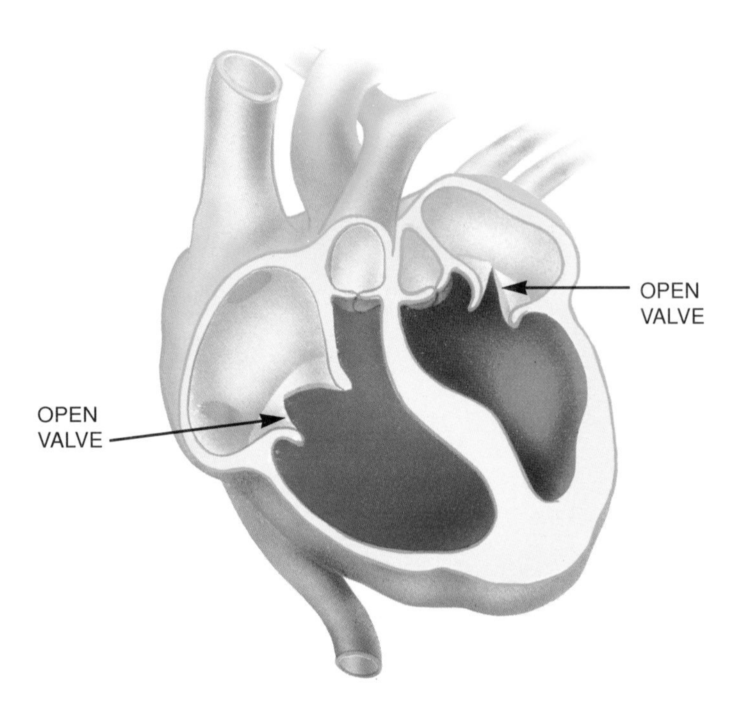

When the valves open, blood in the atria is pushed into the right and left ventricles.

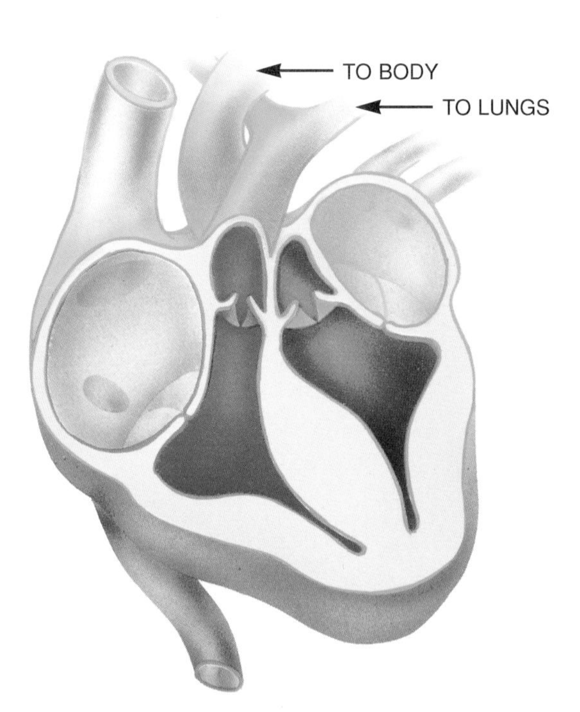

The right ventricle pushes blood to the lungs, and the left ventricle pumps blood out to the rest of the body.

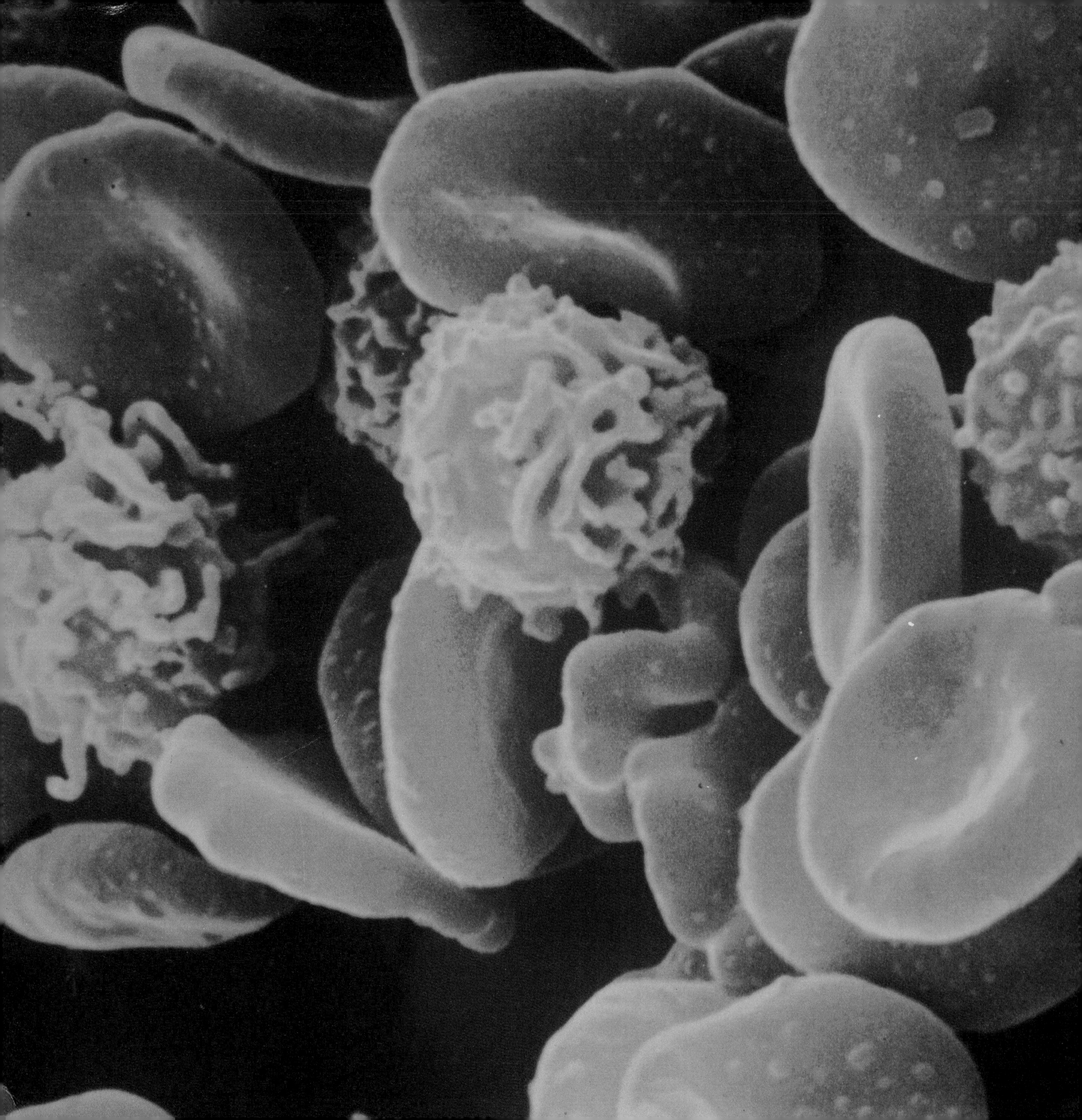

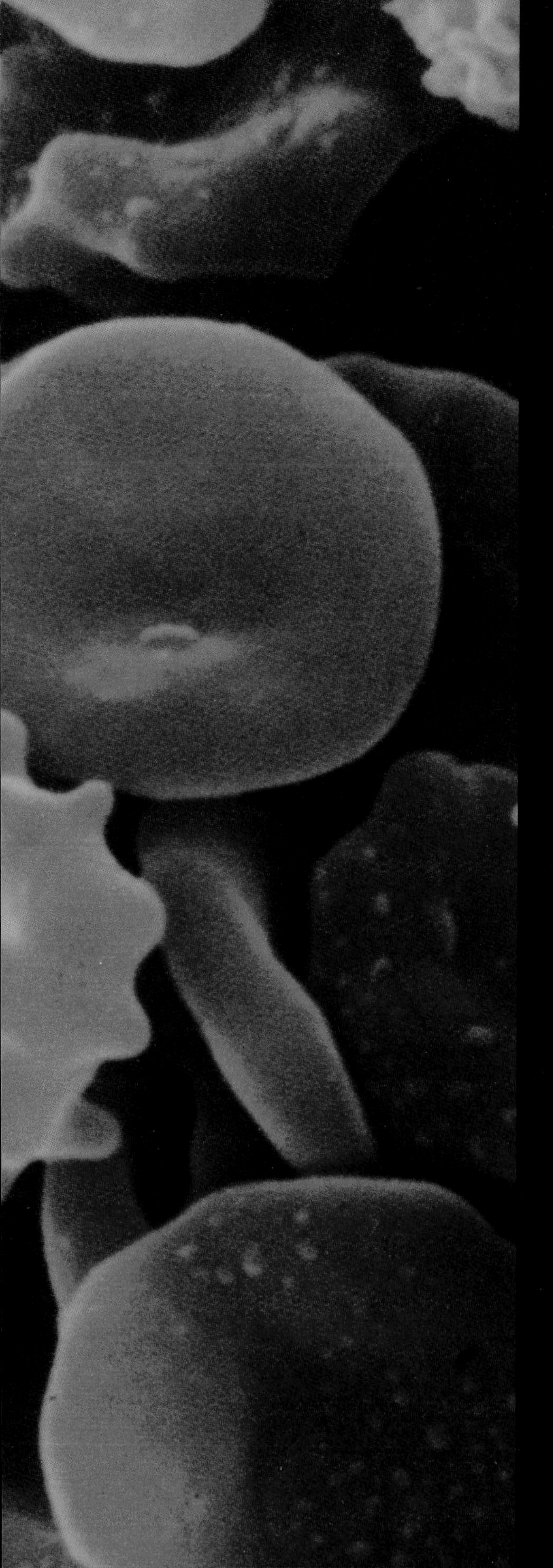

Blood is made up of red cells, white cells, and platelets, all floating in the clear pale gold fluid called plasma that makes up a little more than half of our blood. Plasma is mostly water but also contains many proteins, minerals, and sugars used by the body to build and repair cells. Going all around the body, the plasma carries nutrients from the food that has been digested in the stomach and small intestine to the cells for use as fuel. Because plasma is a liquid, it can pass through the walls of small blood vessels right into the cells. Blood plasma also helps to regulate the body's temperature, moving heat from deep within the body to the skin, head, arms, and legs.

A sea of blood cells enlarged thousands of times is shown in this computer-colored micrograph taken by a scanning electron microscope (SEM).

Red blood cells are the most common cells in the human body. We each have about twenty-five trillion red blood cells, hundreds of times more blood cells than there are stars in the Milky Way galaxy. Shaped something like a doughnut without a hole, each red blood cell is too tiny to see without a microscope. Yet stacked one upon another in a single column, the red blood cells in our bodies would tower thirty thousand miles high!

Red blood cells contain a chemical called hemoglobin, which combines with oxygen in the lungs and gives these blood cells their bright red color. The hemoglobin is the part of the blood that carries oxygen from the lungs to the body's cells and then transports such wastes as carbon dioxide from the cells back to the lungs.

Red blood cells are made by special cells in the spongy tissue of the largest bones, called marrow. Every second our bodies make about three million red blood cells, and in that same second about an equal number die. Each red blood cell lives no longer than four months.

An SEM micrograph pictures red blood cells traveling through a blood vessel.

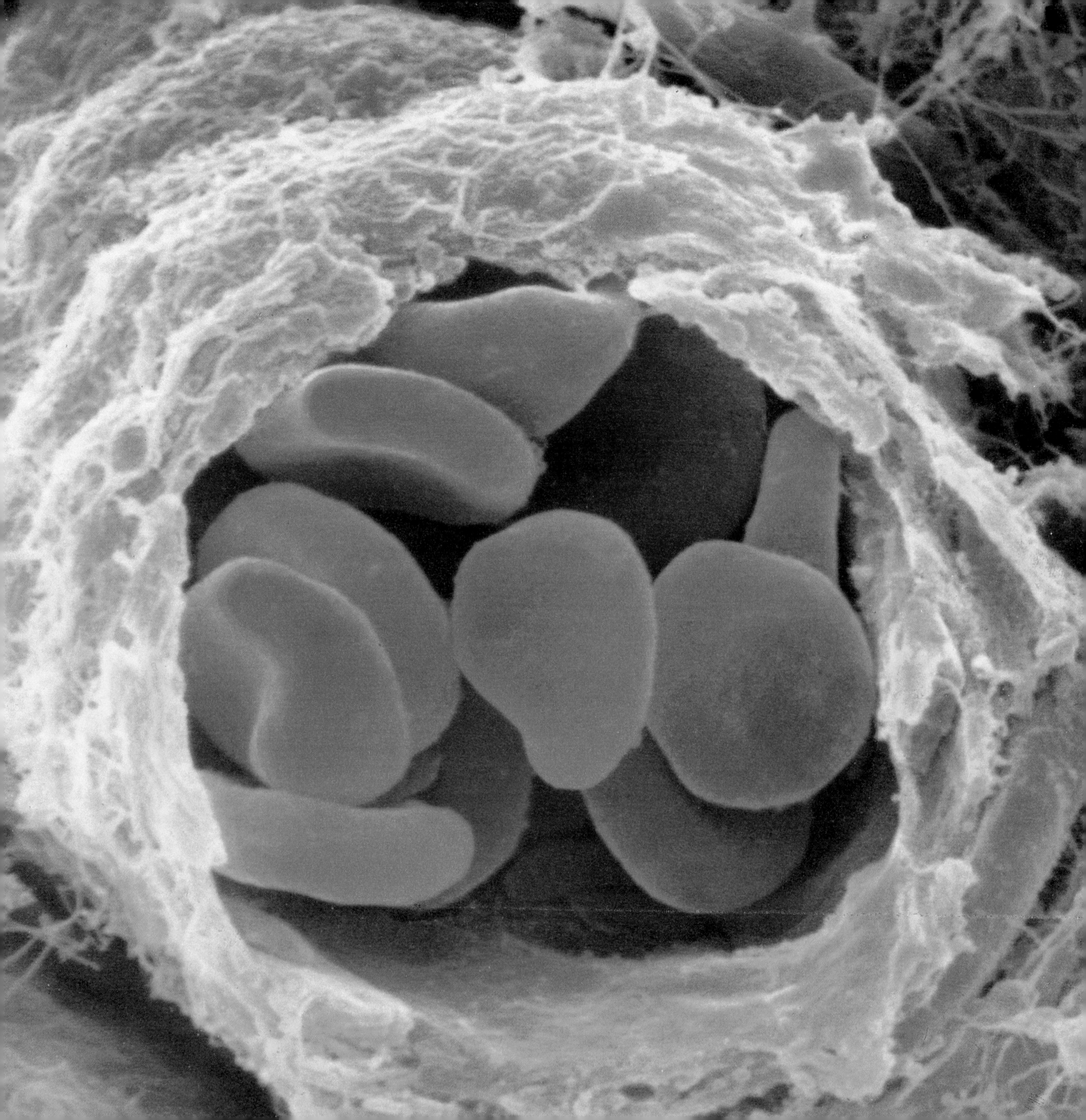

Some one hundred thousand times a day, the muscles of the heart squeeze together. The contraction of the heart is so powerful it could send a jet of water six feet high into the air. As the blood pushes out of the left ventricle of the heart, it smashes with great force into the aorta, the largest blood vessel in the body. This is the beginning of a double journey that will take the blood from the heart to every cell in your body, back to the heart, out to the lungs, and back again to the heart.

The aorta is an artery, a type of blood vessel that carries blood away from the heart. The walls of an artery have three layers: a slippery, waterproof inner lining; a middle layer of elastic tissue and muscle; and an outer casing. The main arteries are as thick as your thumb. They bulge out with each jet of blood from the heart, then squeeze back to their normal width, pushing the blood forward.

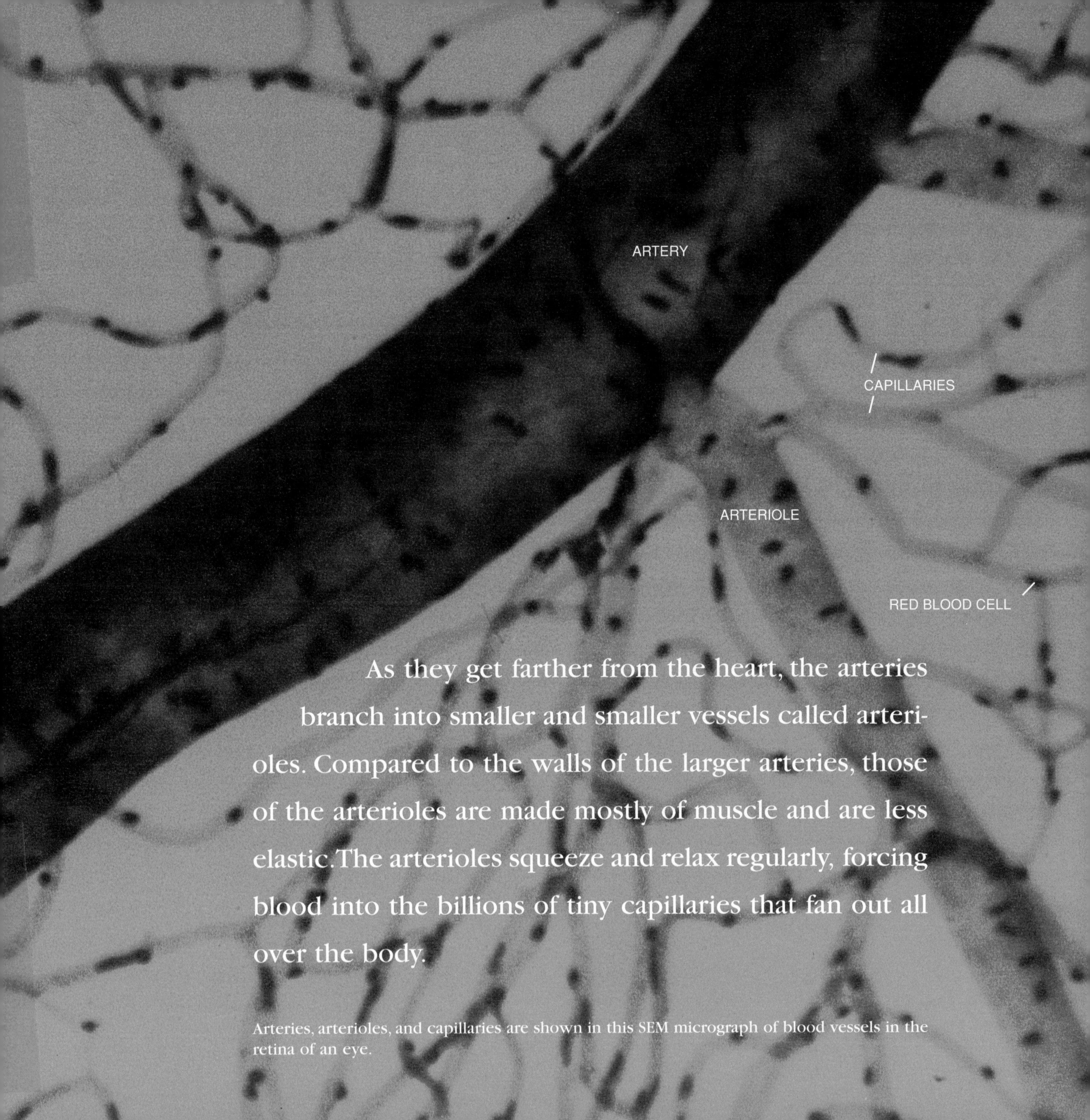

As they get farther from the heart, the arteries branch into smaller and smaller vessels called arterioles. Compared to the walls of the larger arteries, those of the arterioles are made mostly of muscle and are less elastic. The arterioles squeeze and relax regularly, forcing blood into the billions of tiny capillaries that fan out all over the body.

Arteries, arterioles, and capillaries are shown in this SEM micrograph of blood vessels in the retina of an eye.

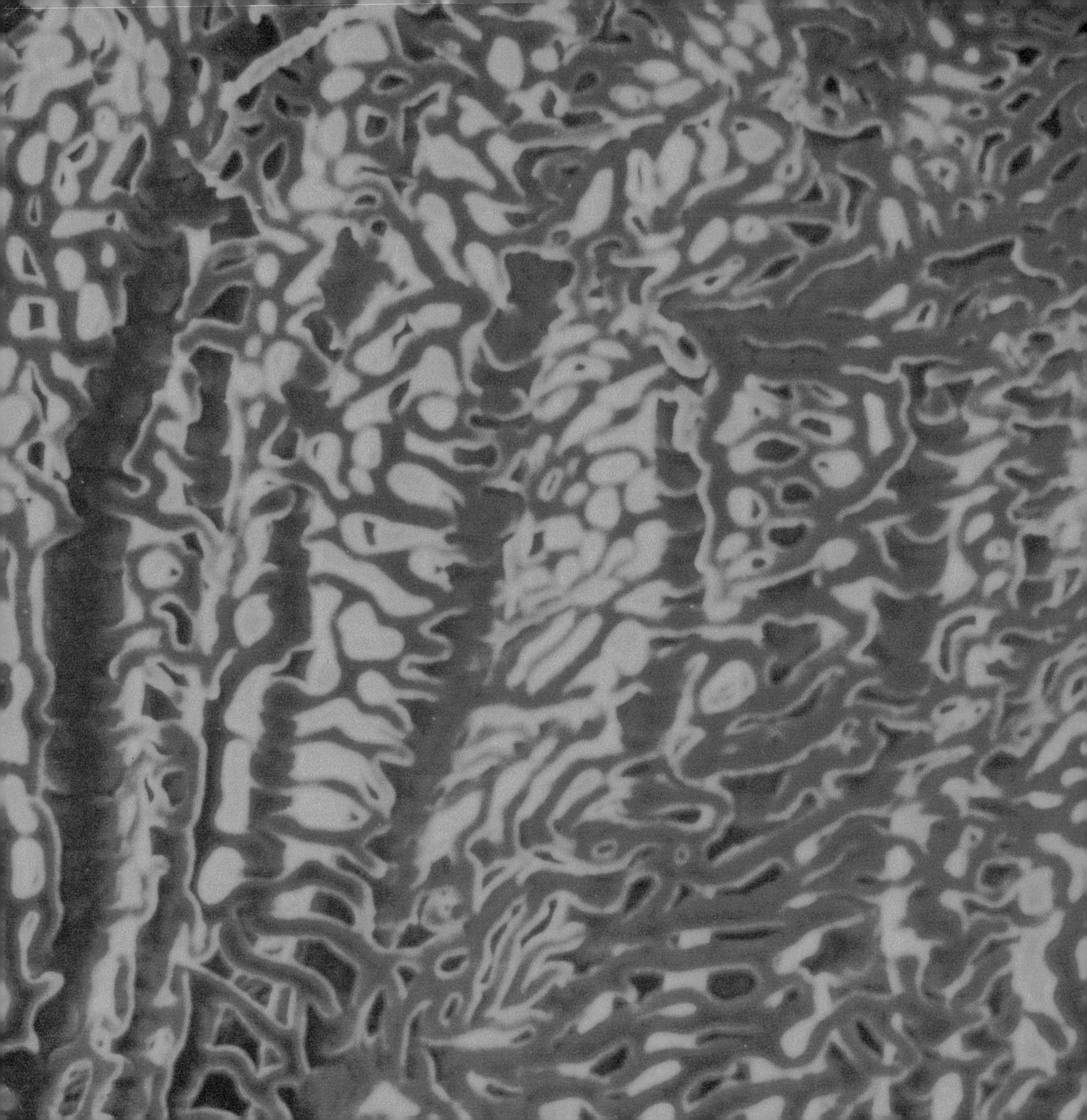

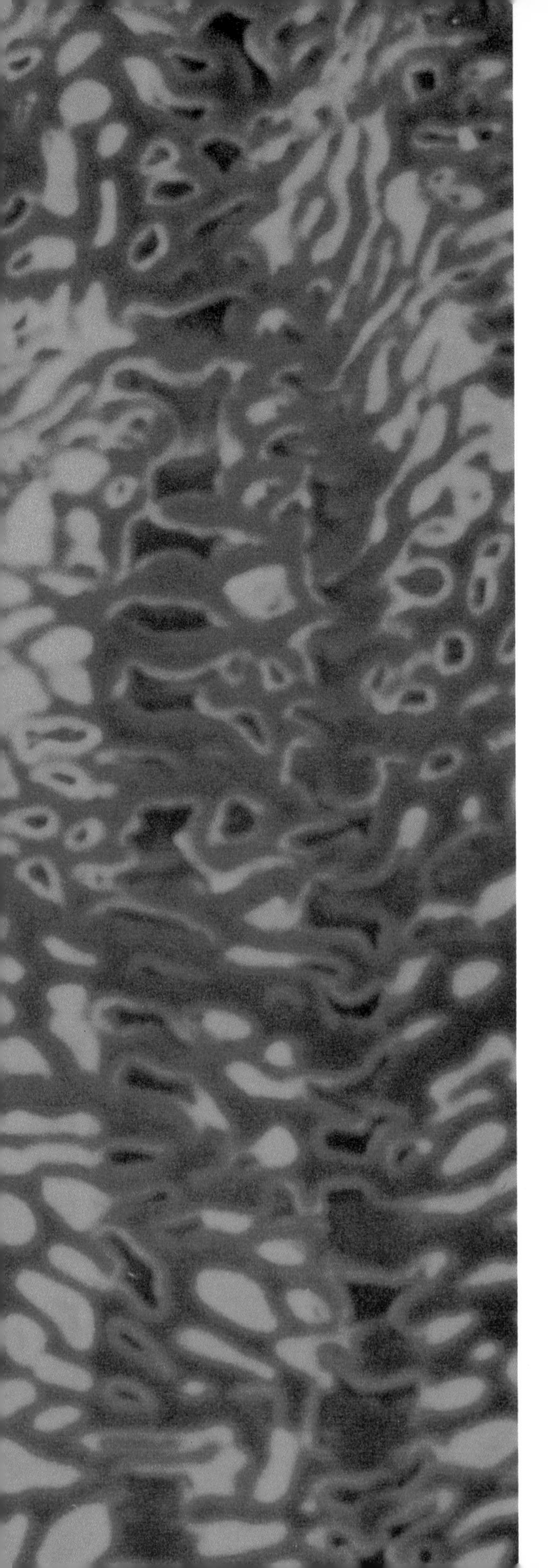

Blood doesn't flow at the same speed in all parts of the body. It spurts from the heart very quickly, but by the time it reaches the capillaries, it has slowed down to a gentle stream. One at a time, red blood cells squeeze through the narrow channels of the capillaries.

In most parts of the body, each cell is only a millionth of an inch from a capillary. Oxygen in the blood passes through the thin walls of the capillaries into the cells. These walls are only one cell thick, thinner than a human hair. Nutrients from food also pass into the cells. At the same time, carbon dioxide and other wastes move out of the cells and into the blood in the capillaries.

A rich network of capillaries is shown here, enlarged hundreds of times by an SEM and colored by computer.

After being pushed through the capillaries, blood passes into small blood vessels called venules, which join to form larger blood vessels called veins. The largest veins are about as thick as a pencil. The bluish-looking blood vessels you see beneath your skin are veins.

Veins, which carry blood toward the heart, have muscular walls like arteries, but the walls are much thinner. Whenever we move, the muscles of our body press against the veins, helping the blood to circulate. The larger veins contain one-way valves that are like little parachutes. They flap open and then close to trap the blood and keep it from flowing backward.

Like the water in streams that joins rivers that return to the sea, blood flows slowly at first after it leaves the capillaries, but then, as veins link together, blood speeds up and comes back to the heart in a steady current. Two large veins feed blood into the heart. The upper vena cava carries blood returning from the brain and the chest, and the lower vena cava carries blood from the stomach and the lower body.

Cross sections of a thick-walled artery (top) and a thinner-walled vein.

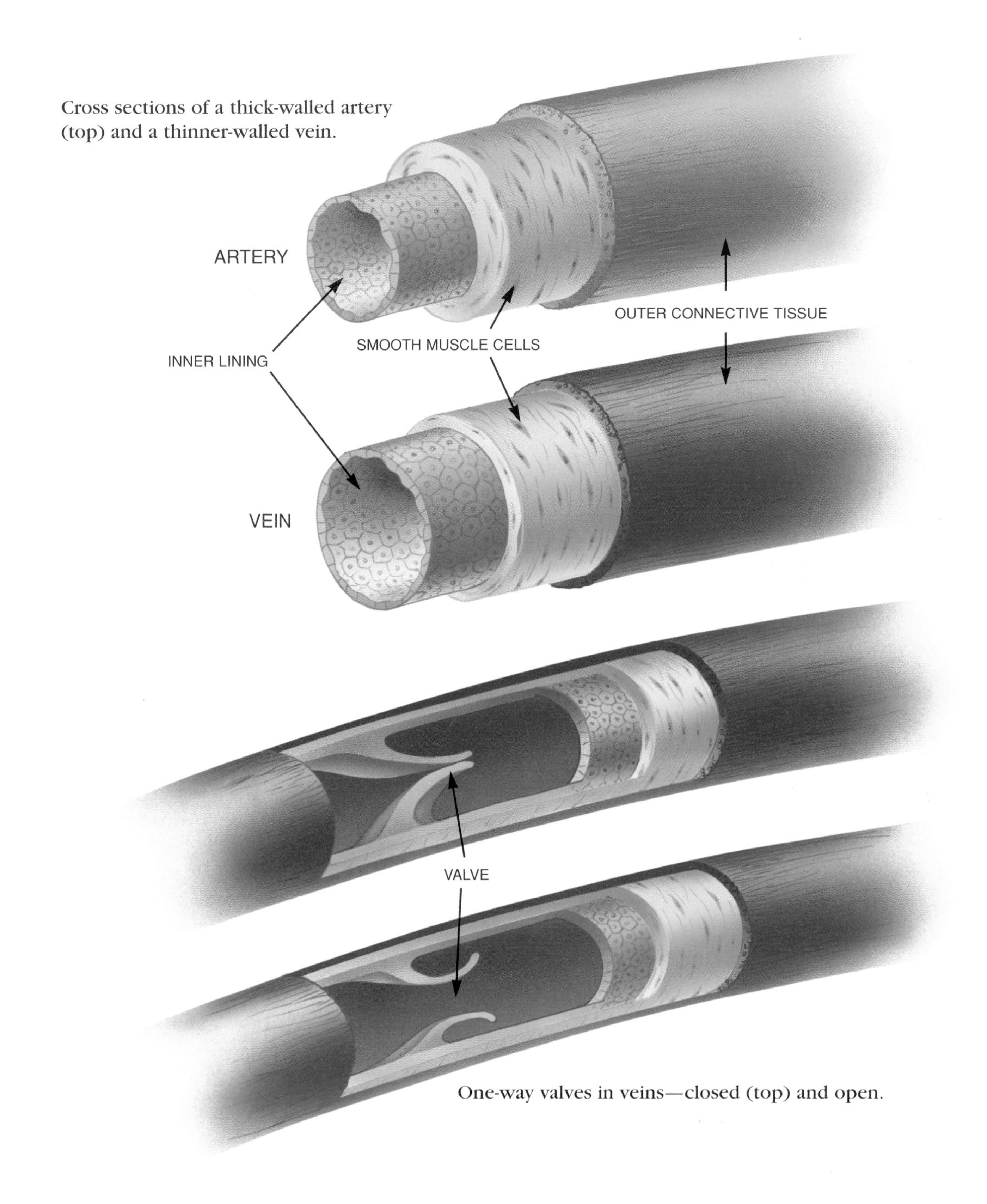

One-way valves in veins—closed (top) and open.

The right atrium receives blood that has just traveled through the body. This blood is dark red, because it has little oxygen. As soon as the blood enters the heart, the muscles of the right atrium squeeze together and push the blood through a one-way valve into the right ventricle. In the next instant, the muscles of the right ventricle squeeze even more powerfully and send a surge of blood into the pulmonary arteries, which lead to the lungs. From there the blood goes into pulmonary arterioles and finally into pulmonary capillaries.

The lungs are spongy, filled with hundreds of millions of tiny air-filled sacs called alveoli. Each air sac is surrounded by capillaries. Oxygen that has been breathed into the lungs passes through the walls of the sacs and into the capillaries, where it binds to the hemoglobin in the blood. Carbon dioxide escapes from the blood into the alveoli and is exhaled. The blood returns to the left atrium by way of the pulmonary veins.

This model shows the great number of branching blood vessels in the lungs

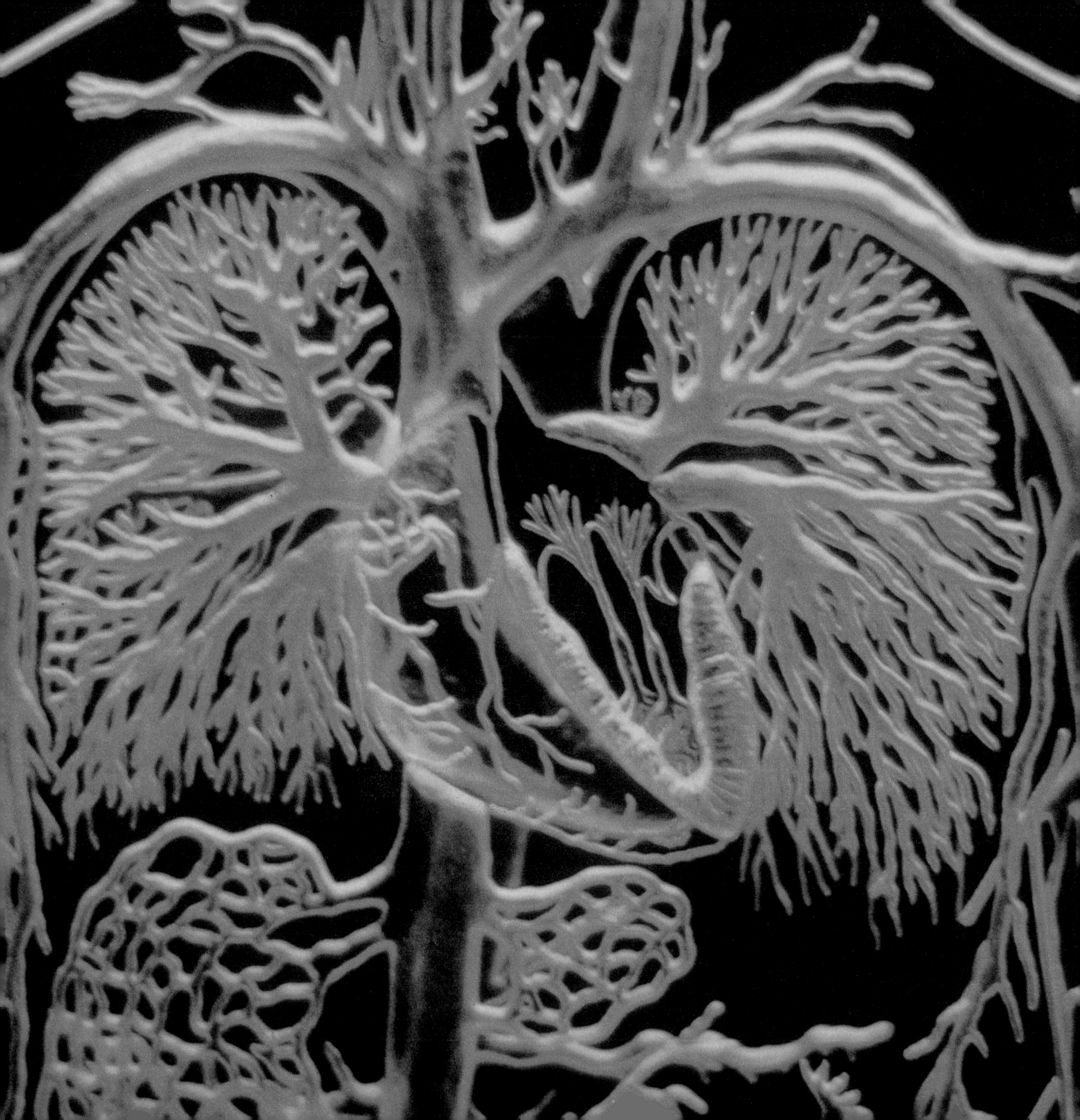

The heart pushes over three million quarts of blood a year through sixty thousand miles of blood vessels in the human body. Our bodies have a double circulation, one to the lungs, called the pulmonary circulation, the other to the rest of the body, called the systemic circulation. Each red blood cell makes the trip out to the body and back to the lungs over one thousand times a day.

You can feel it each time the heart squeezes a jet of blood into the arteries. Place two fingers lightly on the side of your neck just below your chin or on the inside of your wrist below your thumb. The beat you feel is called your pulse. The pulse rate in an adult is between sixty and one hundred beats per minute. Children's pulses range from ninety to one hundred twenty. The heartbeat is regulated by a part of the heart that acts as a pacemaker, called the sinoatrial node. Too much carbon dioxide in the blood signals the heart to speed up its pumping.

A computer-colored scanning photograph reveals the lungs and the pulmonary circulation.

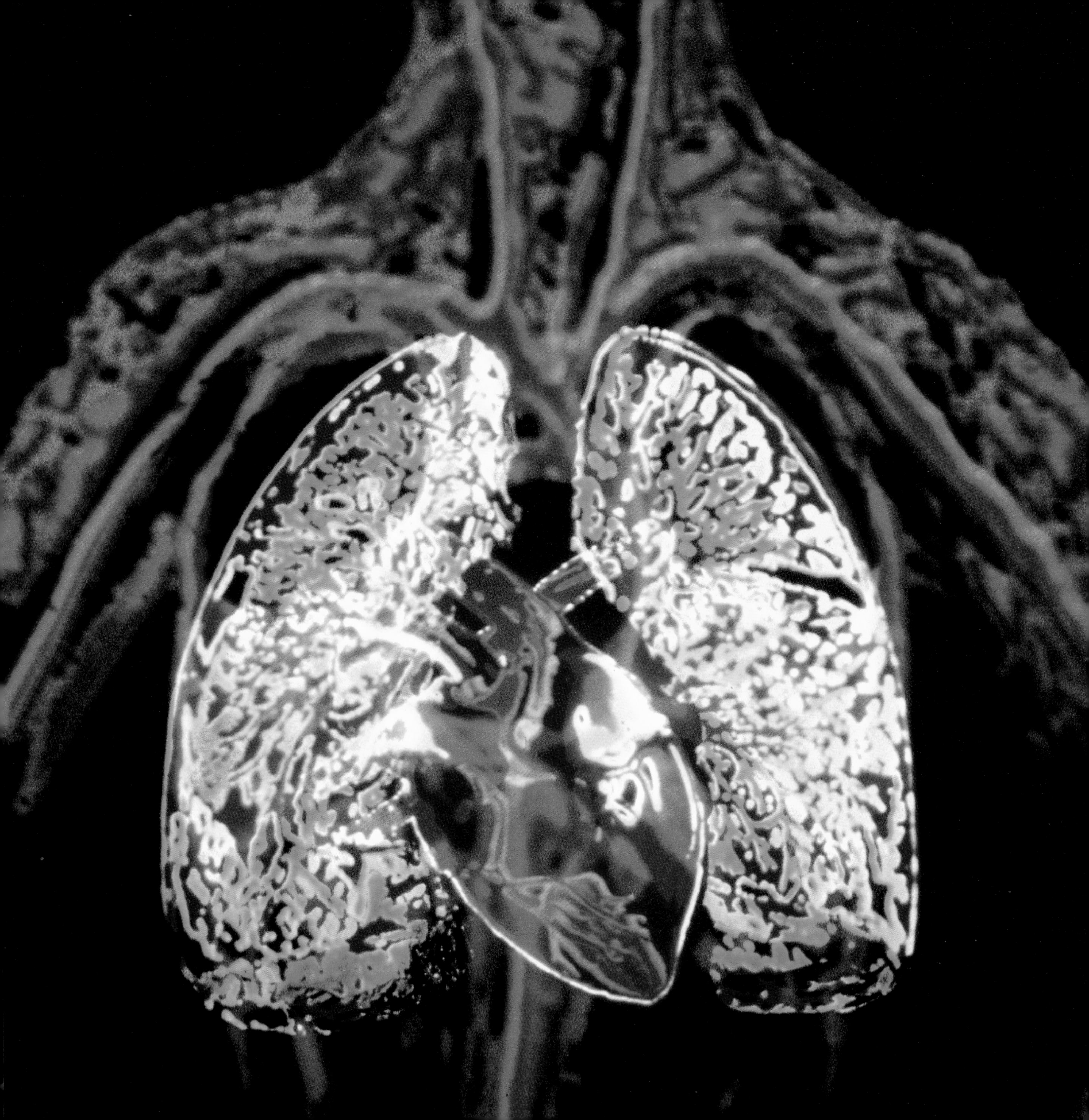

There are seven hundred times more red blood cells in the body than there are white blood cells, but white blood cells perform an important job: They fight disease. A white blood cell lives only about two weeks. New cells are constantly being made in the bone marrow and in other parts of the body.

There are different kinds of white blood cells. Neutrophils are the most common. They are about twice the size of red blood cells. Attracted by chemicals released by bacteria, neutrophils move to an infection and start to engulf the germs, destroying them. The pus that forms at the point of an infection is mostly made up of dead white blood cells.

Lymphocytes are the second most common of the white blood cells and are mostly found in the lymph, a yellowish fluid that bathes the cells. Lymphocytes produce chemicals called antibodies that fight against infection.

Two white blood cells—a monocyte (top) and a lymphocyte—are enlarged thousands of times by an SEM.

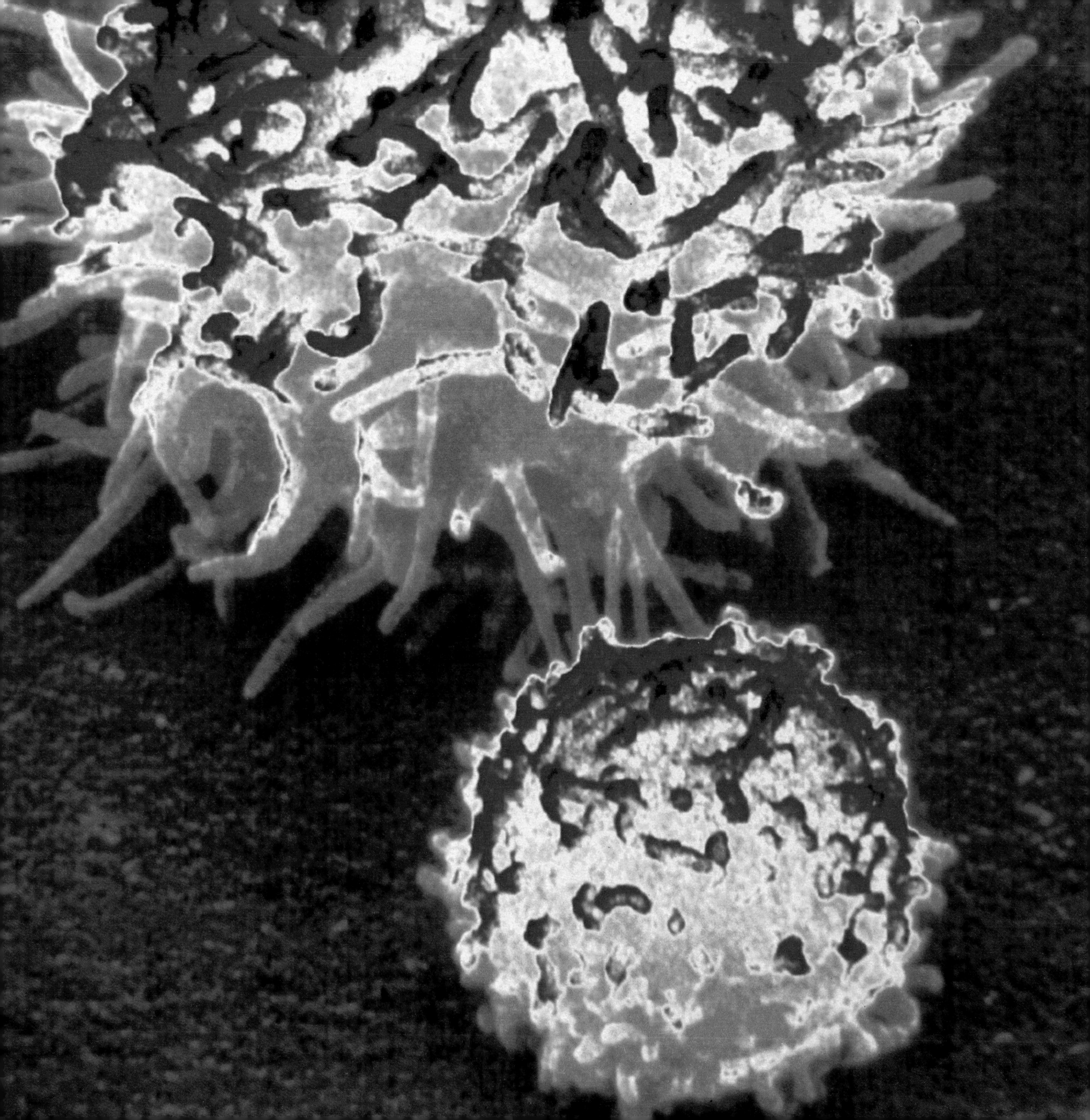

A third type of white blood cell is called a monocyte, which acts something like Pac-Man in the computer game. It moves freely around the body, attacking and engulfing bacteria, viruses, pieces of old dead cells, and other microscopic invaders.

Plasma also contains platelets, small disks that break off from very large cells in the bone marrow. One drop of plasma contains more than one hundred million platelets. There are so many in the blood that there are sure to be a large number nearby wherever bleeding occurs. When blood leaks through a wound, platelets collect around the cut and begin to stick to one another as well as to the blood vessel wall. At the same time, a chemical in the plasma changes and hardens into thin threads of a substance called fibrin. These threads trap the platelets and blood cells, and a clot forms. The clot seals the leak and prevents further bleeding while the cut heals.

An SEM micrograph of a blood clot shows red blood cells and platelets trapped in a web of fibrin threads.

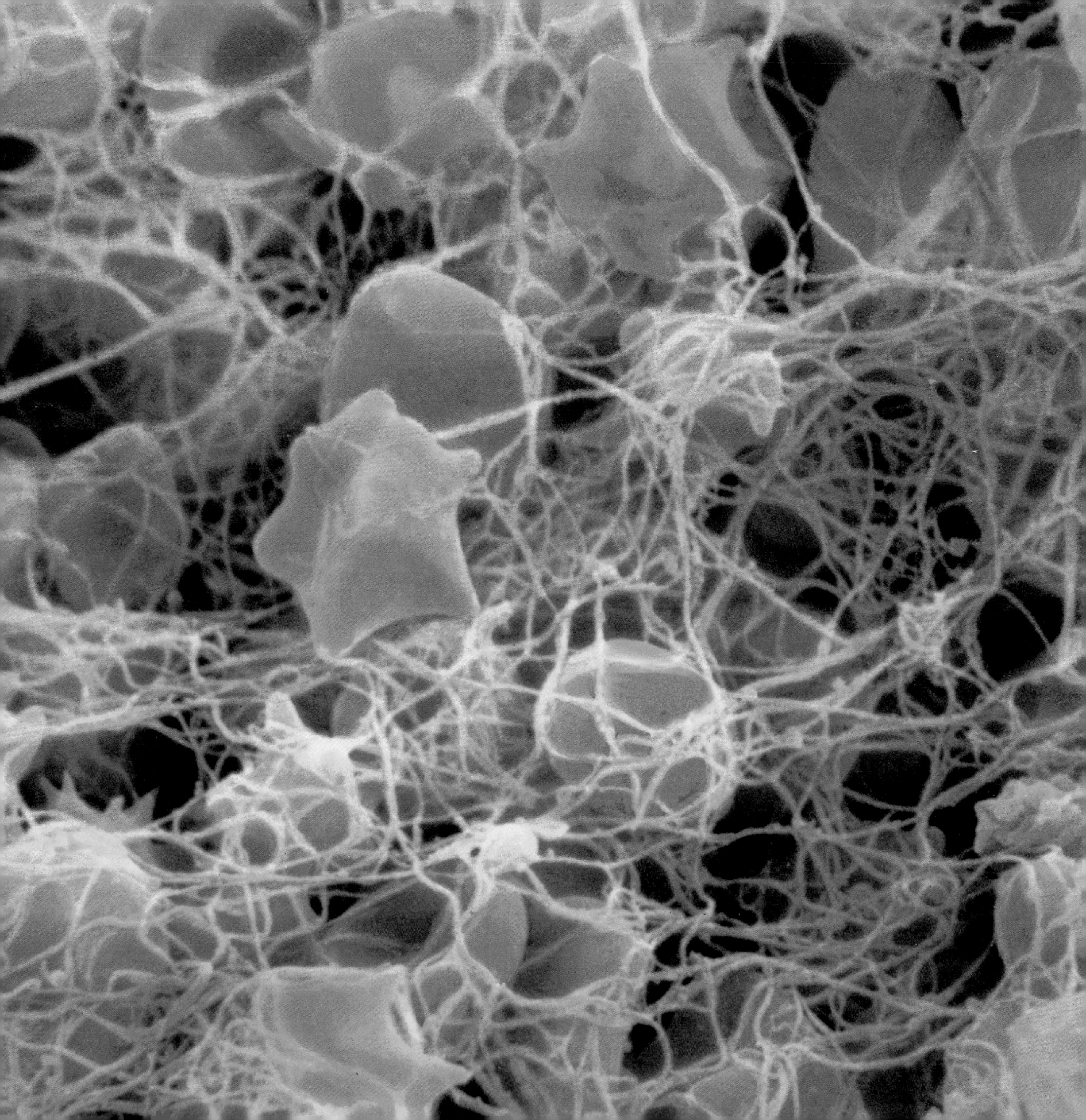

Sometimes things go wrong with the blood's circulatory system. As people grow older, deposits of a substance called cholesterol may begin to appear on the inside of arteries. These deposits, known as plaque, leave less room for the blood to flow through the arteries, and parts of the body may not get enough oxygen.

Angina is a chest pain that is caused when the muscles of the heart temporarily don't get enough oxygen. If the arteries that feed the heart muscles become completely blocked, then the heart muscles will be damaged. That is called a heart attack. But blockage of blood vessels can happen anywhere in the body. A stroke occurs when brain cells do not receive enough oxygen because the arteries leading to the brain have been blocked.

To find out what is happening in the heart and the blood vessels, doctors listen to the heartbeat with a stethoscope and use electrocardiographs, also called EKGs, which trace the heart's electrical impulses.

A computer-colored X ray of the neck reveals a blockage (at arrow) in the carotid artery caused by a large deposit of plaque.

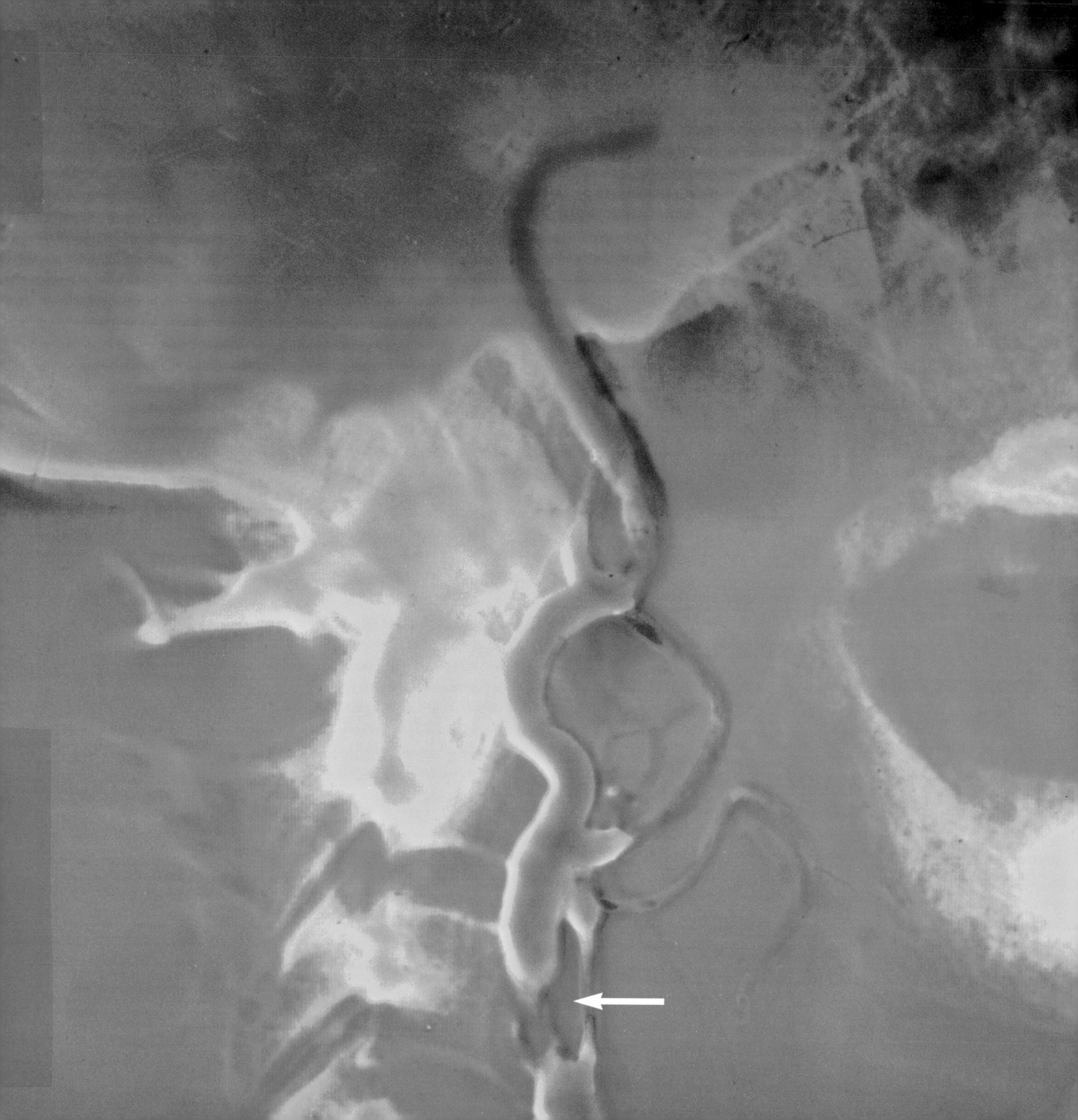

In the past, a person with blocked or clogged heart arteries had to live with the condition. Now blocked arteries can be opened up or replaced. In a procedure called angioplasty, a tiny balloon is inserted into a blocked blood vessel. The balloon is then inflated with fluid for a moment or two. As the balloon fills, it flattens the fatty plaque and opens the way for blood to flow once again in the artery.

In another kind of operation, called coronary bypass surgery, a surgeon adds a section of vein taken from elsewhere in the body to go around a blocked section of a heart artery.

Scientists are always looking for new ways to help people with heart problems. Surgeons sometimes implant a mechanical device called an artificial heart in a person whose heart is beyond repair. They also replace damaged heart valves with plastic and metal valves and use electrical pacemakers to control an irregular heartbeat.

Computer-enhanced ultrasound photographs (sonograms) show an artery partly closed by plaque (top) and the same artery opened by angioplasty.

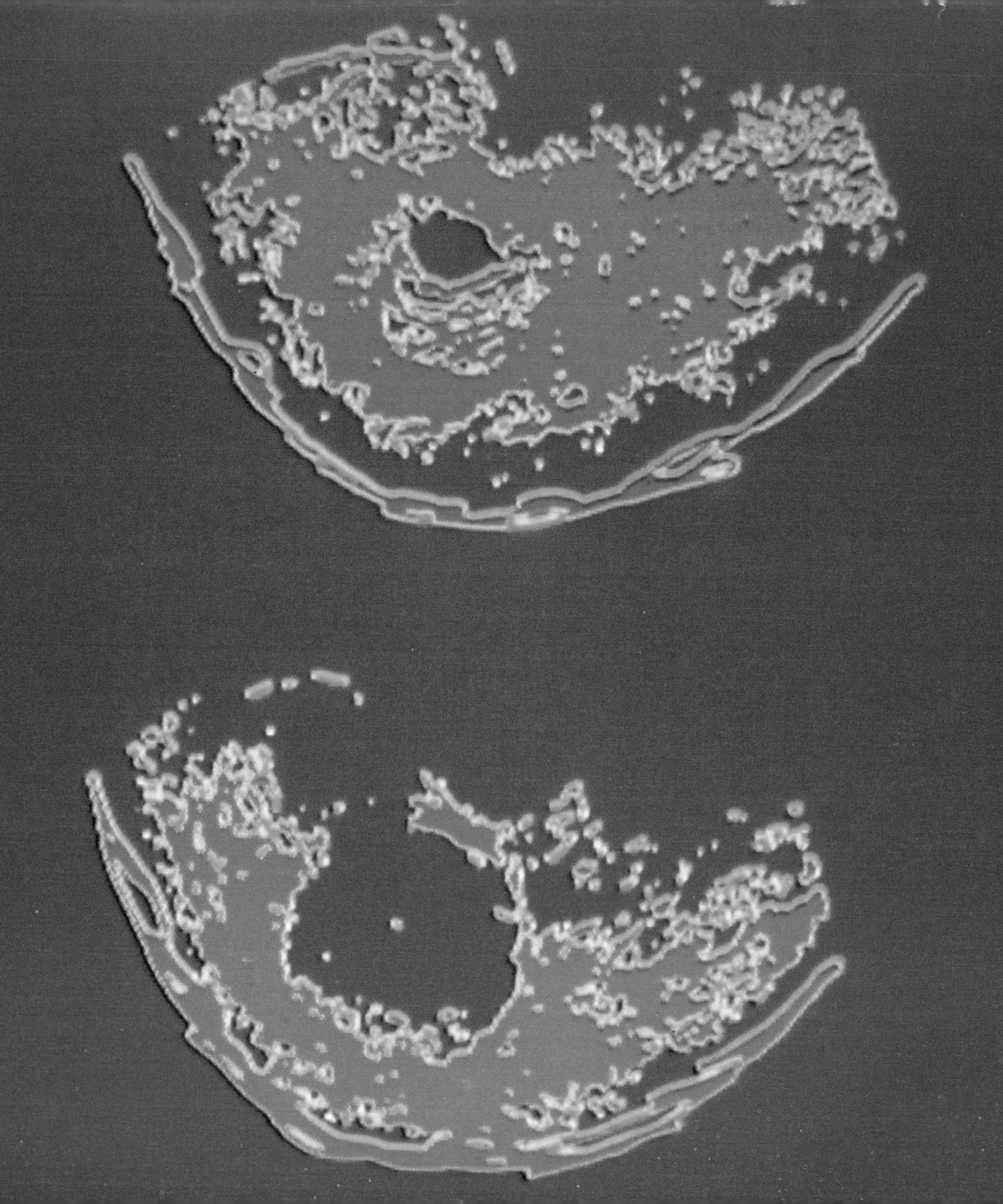

Within each of us flows a river unlike any river on planet Earth. This river of blood flows past every part of the body on an incredible sixty-thousand-mile voyage, enough to travel two and a half times around the world. It is a journey as strange and wonderful as any journey to the stars.